WomensWords

A FEMALE TOUCH

Edited by

Rebecca Mee

First published in Great Britain in 2001 by
WOMENSWORDS
Remus House, Coltsfoot Drive,
Peterborough, PE2 9JX
Telephone (01733) 898101
Fax (01733) 313524

All Rights Reserved

Copyright Contributors 2000

HB ISBN 0 75432 535 0
SB ISBN 0 75432 536 9

FOREWORD

Although we are a nation of poetry writers we are accused of not reading poetry and not buying poetry books: after many years of listening to the incessant gripes of poetry publishers, I can only assume that the books they publish, in general, are books that most people do not want to read.

Poetry should not be obscure, introverted, and as cryptic as a crossword puzzle: it is the poet's duty to reach out and embrace the world.

The world owes the poet nothing and we should not be expected to dig and delve into a rambling discourse searching for some inner meaning.

The reason we write poetry (and almost all of us do) is because we want to communicate: an ideal; an idea; or a specific feeling. Poetry is as essential in communication, as a letter; a radio; a telephone, and the main criteria for selecting the poems in this anthology is very simple: they communicate.

CONTENTS

Bill	Pamela Turner	1
Ghost	Cara Bowen	2
Pig Fat	Wendy Poole	3
Kiss The Dragon	Tracy Gwynne	4
A Smile	Marguerite Longstaff Lowder	5
Born in Spring	Christine E Shepherd	6
A Woman's Best Friend	Susan Davies	7
Note On The Table	Joy Harris	8
Dare You Let Them Out, My Friend?	Pauline Edwards	9
Boy's Room	Trixie Bolter	10
Labour Of Love	Geraldine Varey	11
Tonto	Sylvia White	12
Freedom To Prisoner, But Still Loyal	Elaine Ferguson	13
Old Frankwell	Hilda Brenda Earl	14
Safe In Our Hands	Helen Gilmour	15
Unknown Child - Why?	Jean Mackintosh	16
Motherly Love	Wendy Matthews	17
Trousers	Y Johnson	18
A New Life	Lilian Day	19
Perfect Peace	Janice P Briggs	20
Is Anyone There?	Joan Dambrauskas	21
Forgive Me	Kathryn Gutteridge	22
No Longer Wasting Time	Isabel McEwing	23
Delusions	Sally Kime	24
Revenge	K Mitchell	25
Aunti Rhoda And The Bee-Gees	Hilda Patricia Hanks	26
My No 1 Cause Of Sickness	Samantha Rae Birch	27
Gypsy Love	Parris	28
Damned Dieter	Debbie Keating	29
Women's Words	Pauline Drew	30
Life	F Mitchell	32
In This Day And Age	Pat Fenton	33
Millennium Woman	P Whorwood	34
Ode To Mothers	Tracey Johnson	35

Through A Woman's Eye	K A Barr	36
The Colour Blue	Lorraine Gray	37
The Core	Sylvia Miller	38
Home Style	Marian Jones	39
Once	Sarah Probyn	40
The Brightest Star	Lynsey Calderwood	41
'Day' Ja Vu!	Carol Jones	42
Regrets	Pauline Anderson	43
My Mum Works	Nikita Hill	44
Women's Rights	Faye Howarth	45
Women	Deanne Clarke	46
Who!	Stacy Anderson	47
Famous Women	Bethany Cooke	48
Then You Came	Mary McManus	50
Escape In Mind	Angela Rowe	51
Through A Woman's Eye	Lynn Souter	52
A Day In A Life	Dawn Owen	53
A Quiet Dignity	Valerie Tarbit	54
Untitled	Gillian Coney	55
My Loving Mum	Ellis Waters	56
The Autumn Of My Life	Margaret Tungate	57
Untitled	Judith Macgowan	58
Girls, Girls, Girls	Winifred Smith	59
Mornings	Janet Smith	60
Woman Through The Ages	Jean Godfrey	61
Salad Days	Tania Taylor	62
Dad's Home	S C Campbell	63
Alone	Rose Riley	64
Unheard Messages	Pixie Andrews	65
Creature Of The Night	Patricia Powell	66
My Hug	Marianne Hill	68
Mother's Day Card	Pam Connellan	69
Happiness	Judy Smith	70
My Home	Daphne Foreman	71
To My Daughter	Sheila C Denny	72
Decorations And Appreciations	Stacey Tully	73
Nobody	Jacqueline Podmore	74
Just A reminder	S Snowball	75

Good Intentions	Maggie Nesbitt	76
The Gift	Chris Senior	77
In Two Minds	Gwynne Burn	78
Still A Child	Glenys Blackledge	79
Bless This Mess And All That Live In It!	Sally Osborne	80
Where?	Gillian Goss	82
A Wife's Lament	Marie Angela Bridgen	83
Never	Christina Redfearn	84
Friendship Love Will Never Die	Becky Morris	85
Treadmill	Elizabeth Gray	86
A Woman's Thoughts	B Hattersley	87
Fat Free World	Rhiannon Moore	88
Why Wait	Marjie Bagnall	89
Reflection	Kimberley Clark	90
Battered Wife	Madeline Keyes	92
A Day With My Twins	Jenny Jones	93
Letting Go	Ann Tyas	94
Scans And Mams!	Paddy Jupp	95
The Cross (A Dream)	Violet Mattinson	96
When You Become An Ex	S R Potter	98
Loneliness	K Morris	99
My Mom	Samantha Wood	100
Brief Encounter	Margaret Helliwell	101
Memorial Day	Mair Patchett	102
Youth In Age	Sara Goodwin	103
The Long Way Home	G Ryan	104
A Mother	Jinty Wicks	105
Bonds Of Gold	Phyllis Henderson	106
Dreams	Dinkie	107
Tomorrow's Another New Day	Peggy C	108
Let Our Marriage And Me Go	Caroline Quinn	109
Full Circle	Pat Holloway	110
Raindrops	Kate Rees	111

BILL

Of course
Hillary is loyal -
no self-respecting spouse
would ditch the louse
now.

No captured pawn, she,
of counter-democracy,
or character conspiracy.

Woman-wise
she vies
with all that deifies
and then decries
god-privilege
that satisfies
its human lust.

She will rise,
woman-wise,
as his star
dies.

Pamela Turner

GHOST

As he undresses me in silence
I can feel her presence in the room
in the blue bamboo wallpaper
in her scarlet kimono hanging
empty on the back of the door.

Lips, tongues, skin finally touching
his breath on my face is hers
moving across me with spirit fingers
how her mouth must meet his
when they lie together like this.

I sense her imprint in the pillows
dark hair combed with almond oil
face down as he pounds into me
I can smell her, smell her stain
on the bare sheets of their bed.

Afterwards I see her in the mirror
gliding a brush through long dark hair
and his fingers running through it
like rocks in the path of a waterfall
catching and twisting the heavy spill.

And as I watch I want him again
want his hands to move from her
want to exorcise her from the room
and again start kissing hard and slow
until her shadow withers on the wall.

Cara Bowen

PIG FAT

Pig fat and fetid,
a hammer steals the light;
a swan glides slowly weeping
across the startled night.

Closing doors on starlight,
a shift of velvet steel;
a cracked smile at the vultures
who vainly casts the wheel.

Open heart revealing
a fortress on her face;
a smile, a teardrop, dreaming
invokes the ancient chase.

Pearly armoured lacing,
a mouth to kiss and gag;
a waterfall of daydreams
delays the golden stag.

Gift-wrapped and ragged,
a footfall on the sand;
a journey just beginning
in a child's emerging hand.

Wendy Poole

KISS THE DRAGON

I kissed the dragon's fiery breath
And visualised the devil
I thought of David Bowie reaching Ziggy Stardust level
Though not intoxicated
Nor taking any pills
I felt I'd sipped a potion
As I sifted through the bills
I've read some Harry Potter books
Of wizards not of witches
And watched some period dramas
Of ladies and their riches
But when I'm in my office
I hear the people ask
'Does her face become enshrouded
With a little coloured mask?'
'She opens up those letters
With a blade sharp and serrated
But her mind's not on the job
She always seems so agitated;'
Yes, I kissed the fiery dragon
Sorry did I mean his breath
At work my strange imagination
Leads the dragon to his death.

Tracy Gwynne

A SMILE

How nice to be nice,
To exchange a 'smile',
To say 'Hello'
To hear laughter on a sunny day.
To comfort a crying baby,
Some things we do,
Do not cost a lot,
Certain people are lucky
To be able to enjoy
All the lovely things
Why! Can't we share all,
These lovely things,
To make the world happier.
The sky so blue,
And thoughts of you.

Marguerite Longstaff Lowder

BORN IN SPRING

Don't worry that I am not there in person now,
To accept your birthday greetings, see your smiles,
The sun shines down on me and cast its shadows now,
Just as it always did,
The rain falls on the distant moors,
The daffodils bloom in the garden now, for both of us,
Just as they always did.

Don't worry that I cannot eat the cake you made,
Or open any cards, I read them still,
Their meaning is today as vivid and as deep,
Your love for me as understood as it has always been,
Though I am no longer seen,
The years we had together still remain as real,
For both of us.

Don't worry that you've lost me or that I may have lost you,
It simply isn't true.
I walk the lanes, and ride the winds, and feel the joy of life,
The laughter that we always shared,
And I see you still among old friends,
And hear you talk of me.

Don't worry that they say I died,
Or that you said goodbye to me that day -
I was born in spring,
And like the spring, am never far away.

Christine E Shepherd

A Woman's Best Friend

Just give me a bed
and something to eat
a pat on the head
an occasional treat
a walk in the sun
a walk in the rain
I'll love you forever
and never complain

Susan Davies

NOTE ON THE TABLE

So this is goodbye after twenty-one years,
It feels strange to be on my way,
We gave it our best shot - it wasn't enough
So better to call it a day.

There's nobody else, so no guilt is attached,
No recriminations or fuss,
When the children were gone we found nothing remained,
I wonder what happened to 'us'?

We pass in the night, so I'm reasonably sure
That my going will not break your heart,
Though we're no longer lovers, I hope that one day
We can learn to be good friends apart.

You'll find it quite different left here on your own,
When the shirt fairy's flown her last flight,
There'll be no one to nag when you're drunk with the lads
Or stare at the telly all night.

I'll find conversation with friends I've misplaced,
I'll laugh once again like before,
I've not just lost you but discovered myself
And found I quite liked what I saw:

A person with feelings, her own point of view,
An agenda and something to say,
Not somebody's mother or somebody's wife,
My life starts again from today.

Joy Harris

DARE YOU LET THEM OUT, MY FRIEND?

Dare you let them out, my friend
On this October night?
Your kids might meet a tragic end
Or get into a fight

Dare you let them out alone
Loose old tricks to play?
Frightening old and disabled, they are prone
To be led astray

Be aware of what happened
Earlier this year
In broad daylight on a summer's morn
A parent realised their worst fear

With perverts and crooks on the loose
In town streets and country lanes
Don't let your child die
Like pretty Sarah Payne

Or what about the ruffians
Up to their necks in crime?
Will your child be coming home
In a panda car next time?

You parents! Offer alternatives
As a weekend treat
Make it look exciting
And the trick will lose its treat

Tell them not to meddle
With things that are unknown
This is how problems start
And how seeds of wrath are sown.

Pauline Edwards

BOY'S ROOM

Shoes just thrown
Across the floor
Coats left hanging
On the door,
Towels left on the
Bathroom floor.

You can hardly
Open his bedroom door
With books and papers
And shirts on the floor.

When you say 'Please
Could you help more
By picking your things
Up from the floor.'

His answer is
'Oh, come on Mum,
You must be fair
You know I haven't
Got the time
I've got to meet
My mates by nine.'

Trixie Bolter

LABOUR OF LOVE
(Through the eyes of a man)

Don't give it any thought, it's only women's work,
Cooking, cleaning, shopping too and ironing my shirts.
Taking care of kids, the same thing every day.
She has so much in certainty, but now she wants some pay.
Why is she always moaning, why can't she ever see,
Her job is with the kids of course and taking care of me.

I think I'll have to praise her, or buy her something nice.
The things we have to do indeed, because we've got a wife.
She's looking for a job, well, what can women do?
She'll paint her face and buy new clothes and then join in the queue.
She wants to meet new friends, she wants to earn some cash,
Her friends have put her up to this, she's not that kind of lass.

Things might change at home, if she's not there on time,
What if I have to wait for meals and somehow change my style?
I've told my pals about it, whilst drinking in the pub.
They all threw up their arms and chanted 'Nip it in the bud.'
I've got to put my foot down, it's only right you know.
After all I am a man, she should do as she's told.

She promised to 'obey me'. I know what's best for her.
She doesn't listen anymore, just talks about her needs.
But I'm a good provider, she's going nothing short.
I even mow the lawn for her, I know I do my part.
Why does she want to change things, they're alright as they are.
My mother never moaned at all. She was the best by far.

I bought her a new washer, a tumble dryer too.
Why! Any other man would tell her to make do.
My father always said to me, 'Make sure she knows her place.'
If only I had listened then and not laughed in his face.
But these are modern times and I have had to change.
What next? Is just a wonder, I think it's a disgrace.

Geraldine Varey

TONTO

I have a boxer dog you know,
He is big and brown and furry,
When I take him out for walks,
He's always in a hurry.

This lovely dog is Tonto,
It's very plain to see,
I think the whole wide world of him
And he does of me.

He likes going on the common
For a lot of fun,
And when I throw the ball for him
You ought to see him run.

He always runs so very fast,
It is a treat to see,
And I feel so very proud
That he belongs to me.

Arriving home from shopping,
He waits behind the door,
And wags his tail as if to say
I love you more and more.

I always get him little treats,
It's the first thing that I do,
To let him know that he's been good
And I think that you would too.

Sylvia White

FREEDOM TO PRISONER, BUT STILL LOYAL

Born November '61, oh what fun,
Primary years, through hot pants and tears,
Then the teenage years,
Gary Glitter, Bay City Rollers and discos,
I thought I knew it all,
Then the man of my dreams, still in my teens,
Living together, pregnant and seventeen,
Oh! Is this still my dream?
I've made my bed, I'll have to lie on it,
Split up many times through drunken violence.
I always returned, I loved him, he loved me.
Got married '83 (pregnant again)
No more violence AA took control,
Control of him, and him control of me,
'Where have you been? Who did you see?'
Pregnant again, insecure, unhappy, but still loyal.
'It will get better.' I say, 'it must!'
A good wife, a good mother, I'll struggle through the toil.
He stops working, alcohol takes over again.
No money, no happiness, no nothing, I feel trapped.
Violence again, the last straw, can't take no more.
Have I wasted 22 years? Refuge and kids, but still loyal.

Elaine Ferguson

OLD FRANKWELL

There's many a tale, thee old bridge could tell
Of the millions who once lived down old Frankwell!
And fed the ducks to stop their cry
As rowing boats go swiftly by.

Black and white houses still lean over the road
With their windows broken, grimy and old!
Whilst here and there, the cobbled streets
Still feel rough beneath the feet!
And trees now grow!
On the traffic island of long ago -
Around the fields, there's a tang of newly-cut grass!
Blending in with honeysuckle as we pass!
Just as the heat of the summer day enfolds
The sun blazes down in burnished gold!
Even the old boathouse still stands gazing shabbily
                                            over its land
And in years gone by, many died of the Plague.
Sadly, they went down in unmarked graves.
So when the moonlight beams down and casts her spell!
No wonder the ghosts walk down old Frankwell!

Hilda Brenda Earl

SAFE IN OUR HANDS

Your test is positive Mrs G
and so began my pregnancy.
Blood tests, urine tests, feeling sick
My God! I look like Moby Dick.
Time to go to Rottonrow,
they are expert there you know.
Drink this, swallow this, nurses hover
the NHS has taken me over.
Wake up, it's time to take your pill
It's enough to make you ill.
A doctor appears, assume the position
Relax, it's just an electrician.
Doctors shake their heads in sorrow
Maybe you'll give birth tomorrow.
We've decided to induce
the Labour time it should reduce.
Twelve hours later - no result
another expert to consult.
The machine is on the blink, and so
to the theatre you must go.
A baby girl, weighing 8lb 2
(I feel as if I'm cut in two)
Motherhood fills me full of joy.
Maybe next time I'll have a boy.

Helen Gilmour

UNKNOWN CHILD - WHY?

Why was it we never really met?
On that night I'll not forget.
I did not know, did anyone care?
That a stillborn child I was to bear.
Silent, alone, you went away
Never to hear your mother say.
I love you with all my heart
Before we were torn apart.
The longed-for child was not to be
Why did this happen to you and me?
I've remembered through all the years
With unhappy silent, secret tears
Birthday parties there should have been
But that was just a shattered dream
A toddler you would be now - on the run
A teenager now - out having fun
A handsome young man now - with a pretty girl
A married man now - your head in a whirl
All this should have been your birthright
But Jesus took you on that night
It's said whatever will be will be
Why did this happen to you and me?
Does Jesus keep a tidy record
To answer me when I am called?
Does He take innocent new-born babies when they die
Are they special angels, with Him on High?
Why did this happen to you, why not another?
Why did this happen to me. Why make me suffer?
A reason there must surely be
Why this happened to you and me.

Jean Mackintosh

MOTHERLY LOVE

Take a deep breath, as you conquer the day,
Lots of hard work without any pay.
A day at the shops to find something to eat,
Feeding the family with a budget to meet.
An exercise class is a chance to escape,
A quick coffee and chat with the ladies is great.
The school day has ended, it's a quarter past three,
The children will be coming and wanting their tea.
We sit and play games and have lots of fun,
The hours slip by and now we're all done.
I kiss them goodnight and put them to bed,
And relax till the morning and start over again.
My job is a mother, simply a mum,
A job I will treasure which isn't for some.
My life is fulfilled, a role I enjoy,
It's something I love and will never destroy.

Wendy Matthews

TROUSERS

Trouser lengths have got shorter,
Informs my fashion-conscious daughter.
My mother would term them as half-mast.
The expanse of leg is so vast.
Pedal-pushers below the knee
Make me look like an untidy tree.
Capri pants, now what are those?
I like hems down to my toes.
All ages are embracing this latest craze.
It leaves me in a fashion daze.

Y Johnson

A New Life

I'm in a situation I never thought I'd be,
Back to being a single girl, after years of you and me.
Yes, once we were a couple, but now we are far apart,
And when you went away from me, I know you took my heart.

But now I know it's over, we have nothing left to share,
Only the pain and sadness that both of us must bear.
Yes, a lifetime of possessions, it seems there's nothing more,
Yet I've found peace and solitude I never knew before.

There are pictures in the album, memories on every page,
But I'm now living with reality, yes wisdom comes with age
And now my heart is back with me, I can choose the path I tread
My confidence grows daily, I'm thinking with my head.

Every day as I grow stronger, I know love is everywhere,
I no longer weep or shed a tear on one who does not care.
For now I have a new life, with more meaning than before.
I've finally made a brand new start, at last I've closed the door.

Lilian Day

PERFECT PEACE

Open the door, to who knows where
A beautiful field of daffodils
A deep blue sky, a golden sun
A gentle breeze, and then,
I sit in perfect peace.

Suddenly I see, a river flowing in front
                                  of me,
On the other side, a field appears
Children playing noisily
Loud music from a radio
A boat with couples shouting and laughing
                                  sails by.
Where did my perfect peace go?

Then a voice said to me
'Enjoy watching the children play
Listen to the music and relax
Watch the people having fun.'
Suddenly my perfect peace is here again
Not just for me but for everyone.

Janice P Briggs

IS ANYONE THERE?

Looking upward to the sky
Is God truly there? Say I.
If so, why all the breaking hearts,
Wrenching loved ones apart.
Where is this 'God of Love' I say
         - just believe, trust and pray!
Why *should* I when He takes from me
All I love so tenderly.

A loved one suffers agony.
Why, oh why, should that be?
They said you were a God of Love,
With peace and beauty up above.
        - What good is that, when here on Earth,
You let us suffer pain from our birth?

Watching torture - no helping hand
To help our trauma, I do not understand!
Today no miracles do we see performed.
The raging seas are never calmed,
Your hand is never raised to ease,
Starvation, war, atrocities.

If you hear me, how can I know?
You never answer 'Yes' or 'No.'
Now *I'd* find it hear,
Your voice, your works do not seem near.
You've taken all I loved from me,
And still expect my loyalty.
If you're there, and hear my plea,
Please give my faith back to me.

Joan Dambrauskas

FORGIVE ME

As I looked into your bedroom you were asleep
Peaceful and clean, unaware of me there.
I knelt by your bed and started to pray for forgiveness,
for the day we had shared.
For the guilt I was feeling, when I shouted at you for the hundredth time, the thoughts that I kept hidden away.
For the hand that had almost made contact with your skin; the fury that I held within.
The desperate tears that just spilled without effort but washed down my face like a river.
The anger, the desperation when you wouldn't take your feed and I knew that it was because you sensed all my emotions.
How could you lie in my arms and smile at me when I had spoken such words of frustration?
You deserved better than me, maybe would be better without me and yet we have no choice but to carry on.
Anyway, my sweet baby, forgive me for I love you so dearly, so much that my heart is breaking with the pain.
If only I knew why I felt like this.

Kathryn Gutteridge

NO LONGER WASTING TIME

I woke this morning and faced the truth,
I've wasted my lifetime
I've wasted my youth.

I wove my own net
I wove it so tight,
Freedom wasn't an option,
of it, I lost sight.

Pressure from adults
and my own generation
Marriage, a home, learning
meal preparation.

This was the length of my narrow ambition
a limit was set
my mind pre-conditioned.

Oh for that time,
to be relived and corrected,
For I've discovered a talent
I never suspected.

I live my own life
each day as my last,
No use in the mourning
of things that are past.

Isabel McEwing

DELUSIONS

I look in the mirror and marvel,
How I, mother of a grown-up son,
And with grandchildren,
Could look so young.
My skin is smooth, not a line.
My figure is absolutely fine.
How can my eyes still be so bright?
It isn't only in a good light.
I leave the house, stride down the street.
My heart is light, I'm feeling sweet.
I pass a shop window, who is that old hag?
Is there anywhere that doesn't sag?
Everything is in the wrong place,
And look at the lines on her poor old face.
I think I know her, I give a gasp,
I last saw that face in the looking glass.
Oh misery! What can I do?
I really don't look thirty-two.
But what does it matter about my looks,
When retirement is such a pleasure,
A life full of love, music and books,
And friends I will always treasure.
But still in my heart, and in yours too,
I know we all feel thirty-two.

Sally Kime

REVENGE

Maybe some day I'll wake and find
A world I thought I'd left behind
When I look back upon my youth
I trusted men to tell the truth
But I've gone through life
And watched men cheat
And seen wives turn the other cheek
Then take them back because of pride
Not no one knows how they feel inside
Some bide their time, while others plan
To get revenge upon that man
When kids have grown and left the nest
Then woman comes into her best
She's planned it well, it's taken years
But now this woman has no fears
Her man's worn out, an empty can
He's played the field, his stamina's gone
No female wants a man like this
It's her turn now to take the *psss.*

K Mitchell

AUNTIE RHODA AND THE GEE-GEES

Now placing a bet is Aunt Rhoda's forté,
At ninety-one she sees it as a brainstorming exercise
and not a bit naughty.
Rhoda in common with the Queen Mum enjoys having a flutter
and finds the gee gees great fun.

Auntie likes to rise early, breakfast, then dress and waits
eagerly for the newsagent to arrive with the Press.
Once in her hands there's no time to digress, she follows her
instincts and puts her knowledge to the test.

Runners are studied with much deliberation and soon the moment
arrives for speculation.
Whether it's over the sticks or on the flat, she'll stake tenpence
on this horse and twenty on that.

Rhoda carefully writes down her selection then summons our Wyn
to sprint down to the bookie's, she's a reliable young thing.
Our Wyn, who's a mere seventy plus, will place the bets without
any fuss.

Rhoda now sits patiently watching TV
Wyn plies her with snacks and cups of sweet tea.
Each race she views with great expectation,
and every winner she picks is applauded with great jubilation.

When some fail to make it Aunt Rhoda's not glum,
she's enjoyed the day which has been far from humdrum.

Tomorrow she will rise soon after dawn with her mind focused
on racing and how the horses will perform.
Perhaps Auntie has discovered the key to maintaining her
mental agility.

Hilda Patricia Hanks

MY NO 1 CAUSE OF SICKNESS

Moving out to strain my eyes,
I spiral like gut into mind.
In naked throes of agonising peace,
In clique with similar kind.

Churning crack to break my heart,
I stumble like a drunk into view.
Twisting crunch to break my spine,
A silence with absent clue.

Waiting time extends the game,
I sink like death into trance.
Anticipate risk with guarantee,
A future with blind glance.

Hating you induces sleep,
I try like a fool to succeed.
Logic thought evades my days,
Recognition of stress and need.

Gaping space in exchange for soul,
I'm desperately reaching for closure.
Lonely pressure pounds my veins,
Threatening calm composure.

So, this is me, my arrogant friend,
Do you sleep in a quiet, calm scene.
Nights without you are restless and loud,
So why do you seem so serene?

There must be a way, to lend you the pain,
For just a few moments you'll see.
What you have done in breaking my heart
And how difficult it is to me!

Samantha Rae Birch

GYPSY LOVE

I met a gypsy lad my dear
I met a gypsy lad
When his world lay in ruins
My heart heavy and sad
He took me by the hand, my dear
He led me back to life
Took me into his world
Where everything was bright
He showed me wondrous things my dear
That I had never seen
Opened up a whole new life
Beyond my wildest dreams
I grew to love my gypsy lad
With a passion burning strong
My lovely gypsy lad my dear
To me could do no wrong.
Then they took my love away, my dear
They left me here alone
So here I am without my love
To kiss away my tears.
Now the days are long and lonely
And I sit here near the stream
But the nights my dear
Oh the nights, my dear
My love returns in my dreams.

Parris

DAMNED DIETER

Who put the *no food* in diet?
Who made me see the chocolate and buy it?
Who made my thighs and bum expand?
Who made my clothes tighter than a rubber band?

Who has sent me to the end of my wits
With spicy nuggets and chicken dips?
Where can I possibly lay the blame
For this cruel, heartless, spiteful game?

But I have an Ace, I have a saviour
That I hope will change my eating behaviour
It's helped me lose a little weight
And now I can fit through our garden gate

So I'm no longer scared or afraid
That my husband will have to call the fire brigade
To cut me lose and set me free
'Cause I'm no longer as big as I used to be.

Debbie Keating

WOMEN'S WORDS

From babes in arms
To tiny tots
From ponytails
To teenage spots.

To find true love
And security
To settle down
And raise a family.

First a girl and then a boy
You teach them all you know
From dolls and cars to pretty things
Then watch them thrive and grow.

When first love comes
With all its fears
It breaks your heart
To see their tears.

You pick them up
And stand them tall
Perhaps that love
Wasn't right at all.

Then one day true love will come
You see it in their smile
At last you have a telephone
That's not busy all the while.

A lovely bride in dress of white
She can't resist a twirl
Was this radiant bride-to-be
My lovely little girl?

A handsome groom, his bride in white
Are walking down the aisle,
Despite the tears and a heavy heart
You try your best to smile.

The hardest years are still to come
Now they have flown the nest
Did I teach them everything?
I did my very best.

Pauline Drew

LIFE

Life always has its ups and downs,
Its smiles, its laughs, its doubts, its frowns.
At times, it seems, we're given raw deals,
And we all think, no one know how it feels.
But if we all sat down and gave it some thought,
Perhaps we would realise, we learn what we're taught.
Nobody's perfect, we all make mistakes,
Sometimes a minor one is all that it takes.
Some people can cope with whatever life throws,
Others can't take it, however it goes.
There's not enough time to fall apart,
It's so much better not to take it to heart.

F Mitchell

IN THIS DAY AND AGE

Young women today prefer to be tall,
Elegance doesn't seem to matter at all
The idea being, not to be small,
To be tall, that appears to be the phase
Platform soles are all the rage,
In this modern day and age.

Gone are the stiletto heels and dainty feet,
Which in our days, made one look smart and neat
Graceful too, this, of course, being the style of the shoe.

Women are at the Front with ease
Barristers, doctors, service women, even the Law,
Nothing deters them, progress they have made,
What a wonderful achievement
In this day and age.

When you look around, you will find
Women have their feet fixed firmly on the ground.
Definitely set, come what may
Equality was a good thing in a way.
This they have proved, and are here to stay
It is certainly a Woman's World
This you can't deny.
A Woman's World, as seen through,
                         a Woman's Eye.

Pat Fenton

MILLENNIUM WOMAN

M y husband bought me a gift
I deally to give my spirits a lift
L ogged on, I'm hooked, it's like a drug
L ove this wonderful computer bug
E very day I thank Mr Babbage for this amazing invention
N ote, it's like a woman in complexity and intention
N ow my husband with a plaintive voice said,
 'Is my dinner ready yet?'
I said, 'Sorry, Dear, I'm on the Net'
U se this technology
M otivation is the key

W omen shouldn't be a mother bored, take a megabyte
O nly practise daily to get it right
M onitor the Internet, get to grips
A whole New World at our fingertips
N ext, take a stance you'll make it with the help of Perse-Verance.

P Whorwood

ODE TO MOTHERS

As a child I thought she rarely loved me
Blaming this for my insecurity
Often hearing, no, don't do this or that,
Feeling her hand now and then: smack, smack.
I'd fight and tyrannise my younger brother
Refusing obedience for my poor mother.

Adolescence came, boys, make-up, music and wine.
How can I have fun being in by nine?
A prisoner of youth, I want to be free,
I want to taste life, I want to be me.

Of course - scan the papers, a room to rent,
Hurrah! Leave forever my discontent.
Alas, no boyfriends allowed in my room,
Nor pets, posters, takeaways - what gloom!
Is this what independence is all about?
'My landlord's a beast, oh Mum I tried'
'You gave it a go' was all Mum replied.
Returning home, the rules I then kept
To leave when hitched, my mum she wept.

Wife and mother with a home of my own,
Loving and nagging my kids, Nick and Joe.
Crayoned walls, muddy floors, always drying eyes.
Broken nights and furniture - I did not realise,
How hard this life is of domesticity,
Such insight, yes, my mother did love me.

Tracey Johnson

THROUGH A WOMAN'S EYE

I wake, I need more sleep,
You all cry Mum! Mum! Mum!
Breakfast, help to dress the little ones.
Socks are missing, never a pair of shoes.
Nine-year-old, looks so glum.
Bus passes out, lunch money - just enough!
Uneaten Coco Pops, try not to raise my voice.
time for the bus.
Zippers up, socks are even, maybe tights
would be better for the season.
Pulling at hair with brush, every morning the same rush.
Did you wash both hands? Let me look at your teeth (smile)
Walk to the bus stop.
Stand at the bus stop with other mums,
you don't want to pass the time of day with.
Children, don't forget to kiss me
Wave, smile, hope, they will be OK.
Home and apply other face
And get ready for your other hat
In the childless rat race.

K A Barr

THE COLOUR BLUE

A pregnancy test, the colour shows blue
Preparation starts, so much to do,
Swollen ankles, waistline thick
Every morning feeling sick,
Hormones disturbed, tearful moods,
Manic cravings for unusual foods,
Drinking ice-cold milk instead of wine,
Looking at my reflection, is that tummy mine?
Mothercare rage, never placid,
Pelvic tilts and folic acid
Buying Pampers, teddies and babygros
Looking forward to seeing my lap and my toes
Wearing that tent again trying to look smart
Will those contractions ever start?
Hospital appointments, another scan,
If only I had been born a man,
Time approaching, waters break,
Let's get this over for goodness sake,
An epidural to bear the pain,
To go through this, no, never again!
One final push, the baby cries
Tears are rolling from my eyes
I welcome to the world my new baby boy
Overwhelmed with happiness, contentment and joy
The power of a woman is beyond belief
And when the birth is over, it's beyond relief
Who's the superior sex, need I ask?
Can you imagine a man performing this task?

Lorraine Gray

THE CORE
(Or Lost Cores)

The core of the house is where I'm now sitting
My son would say his bedroom, where secret cigs are lit in
My daughter says her room is, with posters all around
Imagining she's dating the idol she has found
My husband says the lounge is, the tele's there for sport
To sit and view in comfort and pour himself a short
We need some time alone, it's when we all can think
But basically it's then life's rawness we all drink
The kitchen is the place where everybody eats
Discussing many things that we that day may meet
Quite flippant conversation, no subject very deep
But warmth of cosy chatter before our dates we keep.
Yes, the kitchen is the core of many folks' domain
But when the children grow, another core they gain
Then when one's in the kitchen, alone in the whole place
No matter where the core is, it's solitude to face
So keep yourselves together, there's time enough for space
Uniting is such pleasure, I now will rest my case.

Sylvia Miller

HOME STYLE

I look in glossy magazines
And browse through all my books
At projects using my machine
To transform my home's looks
New curtains, covers, cushions too
No limit, it would seem
'Bedroom Glamour', 'Homes with Style'
So fresh, so neat, so clean.
And if you're good with paint and brush
Then stencil, stipple, draw
Change your room in just one day
(Or just a little more)!
Well, if it's all so easy
To make it look so good
Can someone give me expert tips
On how to change my brood?
For, even when I do all this
And my rooms look really sweet
Please tell me why my lads insist
On having such big feet
Which create havoc, mud and mess
With dirt and dust and muck
To leave my décor looking
Like *before* I read the book!

Marian Jones

ONCE

Once I was lost,
In my own pain,
But then you found me,
And made me happy again.

You gave me your love,
And I gave you mine,
I wanted us to last forever,
To last for all time.

I gave you my heart,
My love was true,
All I've ever wanted
Is someone like you.

But it didn't work out,
And we were no more,
My world fell apart,
I felt so torn.

What caused it to end,
My friend and my lover?
You both wanted my time,
And grew jealous of each other.

I'll always love you,
Forever and always,
I'll never forget you
Till the end of my days.

Sarah Probyn (17)

THE BRIGHTEST STAR
(In loving memory of former child star, Lena Zavaroni)

Sitting on the rocks
Looking out across the sea;
The sky grows paler,
The moon disappears.

Too young to remember
'The wee lassie frae Rothesay',
I sing to myself
As I watch the waves tossing.

'Twinkle, twinkle little star
How I wonder what you are . . .'
Up above the world so frail
Your guiding light will never fail.

And as the night grows old and dimmer,
One bright star still softly simmers.

Lynsey Calderwood

'DAY' JA VU!

Monday morning 10 to 9
Must start the school run, quick
Shove the kids into the car
When a voice 'Mum, I feel sick.'

'You can't be ill today,' I cry
I have to go to work
It'll be fine once we've got to school
Plus the boss would go berserk.

Arrive at work ten minutes late,
With hair that looks a sight
My nightmare is to be complete
I'm wearing black bra with blouse that's white.

Raised eyebrows, tuts and whispers
From colleagues one and all
The loudest is 'perfect Penny'
Our office Barbie doll.

A full day done, it's time for home
Get the kids, and make the tea.
A three-course dinner must be served
For them and him and me.

With homework done and faces washed
I take the kids to bed
Time to relax with a glass of wine
And contemplate the next day ahead.

Carol Jones

REGRETS

You went your way and I went mine.
At the time we thought we were doing fine,
But as the years went by I regretted the day
We said goodbye and went our own way.

When I look back it makes me sad
To think of the life we might have had.
If we'd known what fate had had in store
Our lives could have meant so much more.

Pauline Anderson

My Mum Works

My mum works
She also takes me to school

My mum works
She also does the shopping at Morrison's

My mum works
She also does the washing and ironing

My mum works
She also makes the beds

My mum works
She also makes my tea

My mum works
She helps me with my homework

My mum works
She also pays the bills

My mum works
She also feeds the dog

My mum works
She also cleans the windows

My mum works
She also takes us out

My mum works
She also does the garden

My mum works
She also buys our presents

My mum works
Who said women aren't strong?

Nikita Hill

WOMEN'S RIGHTS

Fight for a right.
Put up a fight.
Don't be afraid.
Equal rights God made.
With a right to choose,
women cannot lose.
Whether it's abortion or 'the vote'
women's rights we must promote.
Remember 'Women's Liberation Movement',
'cos even in the year 2000,
there's always room for improvement.

Faye Howarth

WOMEN

Right from the start a struggle we've had
A bite of an apple and child birth is bad

Years of oppression, at sinks women you'd find
Nobody did anything with women in mind

To get things equal be a suffragette
Fight for your rights and the vote you will get

Bad times fall upon us and men go to war
Who keeps Britain running, women galore

The wars were over, women at work is wrong
Go back to the kitchen, where you all belong

By now women have realised they've got a lot to give
They like their independence and finally want to live

We have skills and specialist things we want to learn
To achieve this our bras we've had to burn

We've always had to battle, to get what we've fought for
But to be truly equal we have to fight for more.

Deanne Clarke

WHO!

The tea's on the table
The pots are in the sink
Who's going to wash them up
Who do you think?

Stacy Anderson

FAMOUS WOMEN

Mother Teresa was a caring woman for sure,
She worked with the destitute and the poor.

Nadia Comoneci didn't come last,
She scored a perfect 10, a great gymnast.

Ninnette De Valois didn't dilly dally,
She was the founder of the Royal Ballet

Georgia O'Keefe had a great start,
She was the pioneer of American modern art.

Elisha Otis found things hard to shift,
So she did no more than invented the lift.

Mary Pickford liked to be seen,
She was the first star of the silent screen.

Jean Racine had her goal in sight,
She became a famous playwright.

Beatrice Potter didn't take the slow boat,
Tales about Peter Rabbit she wrote.

Margaret Thatcher a name so sinister,
She became Britain's first Prime Minister.

Agatha Christie went down in history,
She was a writer of murder mystery.

Emily Brontë with quill she writes,
The famous novel of Wuthering Heights.

British Astronomer Cecilia Payne,
Was the first female that Harvard would gain.

Katrina Witt a great creator
Became an Olympic Gold winner as a figure skater.

This space is left free, for you to write your name
Believe in yourself, and you could achieve fame.

Bethany Cooke

THEN YOU CAME

Broken, yet beautiful, it was my own.
But then you came,
But then you came.

You did what you had to, what everyone does.
And then you came,
And then you came.

Coursing through your heart and soul.
The will to live,
The will to live.

You are so red in tooth and claw.
You had to come,
You had to come.

But still I love your indomitable will.
I'm glad you came,
I'm glad you came.

Mary McManus

ESCAPE IN MIND

She got up late, refreshed by sleep
was it today the great escape
She'd made a plan the night before
as she sat on the bathroom floor.
It was the only place to gain,
A moment's solitude, alone
Without the shouts of 'What's for tea'
and 'Can you help me do this please'

It was an idea that returned
when she felt in that certain mood
She had a little ready cash,
hidden for the half planned dash
Would it be by car or plane
she wasn't sure was her refrain.

Her friend then phoned - 'just for a chat'
her mood had changed and that was that.
She checked the time - half past three
little Johnny would soon want tea
the daily routine gathered pace,
she shelved her plans,
without a trace
maybe tomorrow she'd run away,
maybe tomorrow not today.

Angela Rowe

THROUGH A WOMAN'S EYE

As I stare out into space,
thinking about women walking with pace,
They have so much to do,
I wish I felt the same way too,
I feel so lonely, all alone,
Just waiting for someone to phone,
If only I could get out,
All I want to do is shout,
For me being disabled is no fun,
waiting for everything to be done,
If only I could walk,
I would be free to go out and talk,
'Normal' women should never moan,
I feel I have a right to groan,
This is just through my eye,
I think you'll read this and sigh.

Lynn Souter

A Day In A Life

Got up early this morning,
A quarter to six you know,
Walked the dogs, got washed and dressed,
Then to work I go.

Went shopping on the way to work,
Asda opens at eight,
With two bags full, I leave the store,
And carry on at my pace.

In work now by half past eight,
A busy day ahead,
I'll look forward to going home,
And being tucked up tight in bed.

Four o'clock is here yippee,
Now I can go home,
Five fifteen I get through the door,
To my humble home.

Walk the dogs and tidy up,
This woman's work is nearly done,
At last I sit with a sigh of relief,
As nine o'clock has come.

Dawn Owen

A Quiet Dignity

She rests with quiet dignity
Inside her timeless cell.
She dreams each night, life's jailer will
Release her from this hell.

Back through the tangled mists of time
She vainly strives to find
Abandoned, hazy images,
Torn remnants of her mind.

She tampers with lost memories,
Attempting to recall
A name, a face, a word, a voice,
Concealed behind that wall.

A sudden smile illuminates
Frail features, then it fades;
Her face, once more, an inert mask
Behind dark barricades.

Small splinters of a buried life
Fragmented in her brain,
Interred forever in a tomb
Of fear, confusion, pain.

This enemy, senility,
Has thrust his fatal sword
Through fragile links of intellect,
To pierce thought's final cord.

She rests with quiet dignity
Inside her timeless cell.
She knows tonight, life's jailer will
Release her from this hell.

Valerie Tarbit

UNTITLED

Loving, caring is a woman's way
Teaching her children to keep bad thoughts at bay.
Being a wife, a lover and mum
She must be worth a tidy sum.

Gillian Coney

MY LOVING MUM

Mum, I love you, I miss you
So much even though you're gone
You're still in my heart.

The things I would like to tell you
The things I would like to ask
All the questions in my head are coming and rushing past.

Mum if you were alive today
I wouldn't want you to go away
Even though you would be in my heart
It wouldn't be the same.

Ellis Waters (12)

THE AUTUMN OF MY LIFE

The springtime of life is carefree and happy
No time to think what the summer might bring
Mine brought me marriage and children and nappies
Lots of good friends to make my heart sing.

Now autumn is here and we look at it bleakly
A few aches and pains, and joints that are creaky
A time to reflect on the times that we've had
Most of them happy, just a few sad
Weddings and grandchildren
Pleasures galore
Wonderful memories to cherish and store.

Margaret Tungate

Untitled

I'm short and plump,
Not tall and lean,
But there's plenty of lovin'
In this squat machine.

Judith Macgowan

GIRLS, GIRLS, GIRLS

Little girls laughing, holding hands, skipping to school.
Wearing won't stay up socks, black pull on shoes.
Grow to fit gym slips, propelled by fast sturdy legs.
Older school girls, trying hard to be grown up girls,
dressed for a night on the town.
Arm in arm, wearing skimpy tops, surly looks, too much make up
coloured hair, flaunting slender, go on forever legs.
Tiny, ambitious, career girls, wearing painted red smiles,
with pearls for teeth, smelling simply gorgeous.
In smart designer suits, only tottering high heels
Tripping them up.
Mothers and babies adorning a well manicured park
coping with bottles, nappies, prams, toddlers tantrums, tears
Farewell much wanted careers.
Ample figures now eased into straining jeans.
On a bad day bagging leggings
Unhappy ladies families adrift back out there on the circuit
doing the rounds again. Fragile hearts exposed for all to see
Starved for a month to be able to wear a generous size ten
Legs wrapped in black glossy tights all to attract insensitive men
Mature, all alone independent female
Tucked away out of sight in a stifling shabby attic bedroom.
One little suitcase says it all
Cruel Hoteliers charge a substantial extra for the privilege
of all this unhappiness
Must lie down now to ease these throbbing pins
Tired, varicose veined legs standing waiting for the Bingo bus
with a plastic hip walking stick shopping bag need a drag
Watching the children coming home from school
running wild on wonderful strong chubby legs.

Winifred Smith

MORNINGS

Up and at 'em Mummy said,
It's time for school you sleepy heads,
Fill the sink and scrub the face,
Don't forget we're in a race.

Clean your teeth and brush your hair,
Where's your shoes o' over there,
The time it's ticking quickly by,
And now we really have to fly,
Put on your coats and out the door,
Along the road to school once more.

Janet Smith

WOMAN THROUGH THE AGES

In the year 1900 women were of a different kind
Meek and mild not allowed to speak their mind
Up every morning with the lark
Working hard to well past dark
Fires to lay and grates to black
And nothing to show but a breaking back
No hot water until the Aga gets going
Good day for the washing the wind is blowing
Pounding up and down with the dolly in the tub
Once that's done there's floors to scrub
Beat the rugs see the dust fly
Glancing only for a moment towards the sky
The beds are made and the blankets shook
Now it's time for the dinner to cook
Women today don't know they are born
Sun bathe all afternoon on the back lawn
Washing done by a washing machine
Plenty of time left to pamper and preen
Gallons of hot water just turn on the tap
Carpets cleaned with a hoover in a fraction of the time
no need to flap
Dinner is cooked in a microwave
All these things time will save
We can now be outspoken and not remote
We have loads of freedom and the vote
A career of our own and money in the bank
So woman to woman let's be frank
We don't always want to be in control
But I wouldn't want to change the female role.

Jean Godfrey

SALAD DAYS

They say the camera never lies
My holiday pics show great big thighs
I'll have to join that diet club
and cut out all my favourite grub.

I'm so depressed my jeans don't fit
Oh how I need a chocolate hit
I tried that windy cabbage diet
very organic but not very quiet.

I really should try and exercise
can't have burgers, can't have fries
Little pickers wear bigger knickers
How mum's words were very wise.

Stomach grumbles through the night
Can't I just accept my cellulite?
It's only breakfast, I've had all my sins
I'm like a whale minus the fins.

I've got to try and shift this flab
When Christmas comes I'll look fab
I've lost a pound, I'm on low fat crisps
Does my bum look big in this?

Tania Taylor

DAD'S HOME

The smell of other people and aftershave on his suit.
'Hello!'
My friends think he's great,
he's funny,
I'm proud.
He's seen lots of clients,
made lots of money,
he's happy.
He tells a joke,
chats to my mum,
drinks some tea.
A clever man . . . I'm proud.
Dad's home.

The smell of smoke, alcohol and perfume on his suit.
No 'Hello.'
My friends are asleep now, it's late
I'm scared.
He's seen lots of friends,
drank lots of Whiskey,
he's drunk.
He starts a row,
hits my mum,
drinks some whiskey.
A clever man . . . I'm scared.
Dad's home.

S C Cambell

ALONE

An only child
Secluded, as I grew
One girl amongst a street full of boys
Shunned and tormented
Because of my gender
Moving from village to town to city
I knew no one
I reached out and found someone
Or at least so I thought
Someone who cared
Wrong!
Two tiny children and me
Alone again
My parents left
They passed away
No more family to care
Friends? Yes,
But not close enough to understand
The sorrow, the grief and emptiness I feel inside,
When the children are not there.
At home, once more I sit alone
No one visits
No adult conversation
Just solitary confinement
Though I've committed no crime
Isolated.
How long must I live in solitude
An only child
Alone

Rose Riley

UNHEARD MESSAGES

Within the tangled web of life we weave,
There are often messages we don't perceive,
But, when eventually we give them attention,
They give us life energy from a different dimension.

So from unheard thoughts and dreams,
We find feelings trickling through in streams,
With this in mind, sweetheart I dare,
Wade in, who knows you may find someone who'll care.

Along the path of life together we could go,
Discovering along the way all there is to know,
Of life's great wonders from above,
Peace, tranquillity, happiness and love.

Pixie Andrews

CREATURE OF THE NIGHT

At night, whilst most were sleeping, the Creature crept from her lair
though safe and warm it protected her, by day she wouldn't have dared.
She planned her journey carefully, those humans to avoid,
She couldn't afford them seeing her, she wasn't a humanoid.

No longer a mate to protect her, could she survive now, all alone
That poor creature who was suffering, poor creature, all alone.
With darting eyes she scurried, only taking what she need,
Frightened and bewildered, a pitiful sight indeed.

Without a mate to follow only her instincts now could lead,
That poor creature, so sore wounded, bolting home at fastest speed.
Safe in her lair she huddled. Safe from hate and harm. Licking her
wounds and whimpering, when instinct rang alarms.

Hunted still by humanoids, yet once so proud to be.
Poor creature, she was dying. Why couldn't they let her be?
What a shock when they finally found her. Poor creature
so desperately thin.
Euthanasia would have been kinder. With the terrible state she was in.

Her bones protruded disturbingly. Her eyes all matted, couldn't see.
Frightened and whimpering pitifully. 'They' couldn't leave her you see.
So 'They' took her away for 'treatment.' They thought they
were being kind.
With patience, care and medicines, her wounds they tried to bind.

And when the 'Healing' was all completed. 'They' put her on display.
The world could marvel at their skill. And the creature
could pay her way.
But she wanted to be free of 'existing.' To have died with dignity.
That's the way in the animal kingdom. 'Cept that Creature
was really me!

In this world of 'human kindness,' with moral principles strongly held
'They' are forced to save you from yourself, and condemn you to
this living hell.

Patricia Powell

MY HUG

If I could scoop you all up,
and squeeze you so hard,
My hug would just say it
And you would just know.

So many to mention
Too often, the same:
Friendships, they ebb and flow
and some eventually wane.

I never forget how precious, each one
How 'in debt' and honoured, for all our shared fun.

On end of world night skies,
I rehearse premature 'Goodbyes'
What would I say to measure my thanks?
I can't tell you, my friends
Just how special you are
But to hug you with no words -
One hug would go far.

Marianne Hill

MOTHER'S DAY CARD

After lunch came the best part of the day
When we made tracks and tunnels out of cool damp sand
Or took our turn in the Wendy house with its real black phone
And miniature pots and pans and pretty gingham curtains
Which Miss Frith had made from the remnants bag.
But today, she said brightly, as we eyed with interest
The coloured card and the stumpy pots of paint
We are going to make a beautiful Mother's Day card!
I bit my lip, a bit pink, but curious rather than dismayed.
Would she remember? Could I make mine for a grandma instead?
Politeness kept back the awkward question
And everyone else was already snipping and pasting with
tongue-pointed care.
It seemed easier to go along with it.
And although Miss seemed to sense my heart wasn't in it,
Especially writing 'To Mummy with love,' I did my best.
I placed it, still sticky, in my satchel and walked home thoughtfully
on a cold afternoon.
A bold decision as I approached an open bin; I scrunched it up and
dropped it in.
That felt better.
Back home, I skipped through the back door and sniffed with delight
warm fairy cakes.
A hug from Grandma and a glass of pop.
What did you do today, chick? It was easier to fib.
I made her a nice card, at home, which took pride of place on top
of the TV.
Dad was impressed when he saw it, and relieved, I could tell.
Years later, all the letters my children bring home start
'Dear Parents, Guardians and Carers,' and I'm glad to see it,
Remembering my hot face all those years ago
Dreading an explanation that would mark me out and noting
with unease
That kindly Miss Frith didn't know as much as I'd thought she did.

Pam Connellan

HAPPINESS

Happiness is a state of mind
Which I dare not touch, in case I find
It evaporate in the summer sun
And desecrate other things to come
One golden day I felt it's touch
The sun and sea were just too much
To bear, their beauty so intense
As I lingered there, by the top field fence
My dogs sprawled out, with lolling tongue
Envisaging the walks to come
And across my mind in boldest text
I am Happy, what came next?
In the evening my mother died
My soul expired with the tide
Now, if happiness breaks on a wave of elation
I fear it may be the creation
Of grief and sorrow
Joy today, and pain tomorrow.

Judy Smith

MY HOME

'Wouldn't touch it with a barge pole,'
So the agent said
And my hopes of owning a house of my own
Almost nearly fled:
But my heart was set upon it,
So I tramped around, cap in hand,
Until at last I succeeded
And I bought my 'promised land.'

The roof was undulating,
The floor joists all gave way,
And the outlook was blocked by a mighty shed,
But I did not dismay:
With a load of imagination
And a lot of hard work too,
Out of the almost derelict
My little dream-house grew.

Now it isn't a wonderful palace,
And it has its drawbacks still,
But it's snug and warm and the garden a joy,
Where the sunny hours we fill:
Now my cat and I in the garden browse,
Of our little back-street terrace house.

Daphne Foreman

TO MY DAUGHTER

Is this the little dark-haired girl
Who used to run and hide
Standing here before me
A beautiful millennium bride.

How did you grow so quickly,
The years have simply flown
Now you're leaving with your husband
To make a life of your own.

We have always been good friends
In everything we do
And now you leave the little nest
Part of me goes too.

And if you have a little girl
I hope that she will be
A daughter to be proud of
As close as you and me.

We wish you every happiness
Long life, good health and cheer
And please remember one thing,
That we are always here.

As you go throughout your life
Be faithful to each other
For there is no better relationship
Than a daughter and her mother.

Sheila C Denny

DECORATIONS AND APPRECIATIONS

We never sang round the piano,
or pinned our stockings high,
never waited by the window,
to see *Santa* in the sky.

The Gifts were always wrapped so well,
Never laid below the tree,
Because there never was enough room,
For the eldest, middle and me.

Still we were all so grateful,
we laughed and played all day,
My parents made this happen,
It's because they love us all. . .I say.

They scrimped and saved and did without
My mother cooked our meal,
They did the best they could,
To keep our 'Hero' real.

There is no such thing as 'Santa.'
Even when we knew,
My parents made Christmas special,
Just like they always do.

Still a tree and decorations,
still music, gifts and food,
They kept that Christmas spirit,
And shared it best they could.

So thank you Mum and Dad
I will remember always,
and because of you my children,
Will have the happiest Christmas too.

Stacey Tully

NOBODY

When you're gone I'll miss the naked warmth of your body
against mine
chest, arms, legs
No more will your rough large hands caress me
Firm, fingers, strokes
I'll no longer feel your warm moist lips against mine
Moving, moist, soft
Only friends and children will kiss me
Just to say Hello or Goodbye
peck, peck, peck
What will I do when there's nobody for my body.

Jacqueline Podmore

JUST A REMINDER

Hope you like your new lunch box
I know I look quite small
But Sandwiches, biscuits, eggs and fruit,
I can hold them all!
With love and care I should last a while
So you could always lunch in style,
When work is over and it's time to go
Please don't leave me all alone
Clear your desk, turn off the phone
Don't forget to pick me up and take me home.

S Snowball

GOOD INTENTIONS

This is the day of a new beginning,
I'm going to change my style,
All the chores I've started and left
Will be finished, not left in a pile.

The ironing I keep hiding away,
Will be brought out and pressed, I swear,
The cupboards I keep meaning to clear,
Will be tidied and left quite bare.

I'm going to change,
I'll make a clean sweep,
I promise myself each day,
Then I find in the cupboard
Old photos, old toys,
My child's wings from a Nativity play.
I can't throw them out,
So back it all goes,
I'll do it, I promise, some day!

Maggie Nesbitt

THE GIFT

A wonderful gift; A joy surpassing the freshness of creation.
Pleasure and pain are one and the same: the radiance of all that shines;
Now we two are part of each other.
Out of love for you I bore a son.
Thank you for this precious gift; A jewel amongst perfections riches.
Only and once are one and the same: the ancient mystery of all
                                            that shines.
Our story reaches its final chapter;
Out of love for you I bore a son.

Chris Senior

IN TWO MINDS

Emma

I wonder what you're thinking, Mum, when you smile your tired smile?
I want to talk to you, my mum, but you're so busy all the while
I really want to tell you, Mum, of my life that's changed so much
Life at university, Mum, but you only tell me 'Shush'.

You're looking very weary, Mum, you've been working all the week
But now you're home beside me, Mum, it's your company I seek
I'm going back to uni, Mum, I'll not be home 'til June
Please talk with me just once, dear Mum, I'm leaving very soon.

I'm sitting now beside you, Mum, you've noticed that I'm here
You smile so warmly at me, Mum, and say 'What is it dear?'
We sit and talk together, Mum, but now you need to make the tea
But thank you for that cuddle, Mum, and the time you've spent
                                                                    with me.

Mum

Ah, there you are my darling, you've crept in like a cat
I just need to get my sewing done then we can have a chat
I'm feeling rather tired dear, there's so much I have to do
I wish I had a bit more time so I could talk to you

I thought I heard you earlier but when I turned around
You'd crept away so silently, you hardly made a sound
But you're going back to uni soon and you know we've never had
a chance to have a natter, pet, it makes me rather sad

The meal can wait, the housework's done, the sewing's put away
Come here my love, and cuddle in, what do you need to say?
An hour's past so quickly dear, now I need to make the tea
But thank you darling, for being you, and spending time with me

Gwynne Burn

STILL A CHILD

Those young girl's dreams
Have passed away
Yet I still feel the child.
The mother of two, a girl and a boy
They caused me pain and brought me joy.
Yet I still feel the child.
I long for the days when I was free
The young men calling round for me.
I long for the bright lights shining on
And I know those days have long since gone.
Yet I still feel the child.
My children cry, I wipe the tears,
I'm crying too but no one hears.
You may see the woman,
Yet I still feel the child.

Glenys Blackledge

BLESS THIS MESS AND ALL THAT LIVE IN IT!
(Dedicated to Toyah, Lymarah and Billy)

Looking around here you may think what a mess,
honestly I have little time to rest.

I wipe many a tear over grazed knees, 'Mummy can I have this please'

Getting them dressed and ready for school,
I get in a fluster and feel such a fool.

Up to school in all sorts of weather, sometimes I come
to the end of my tether!

Then back home to tidy up, the youngest is such a mucky pup!

Then comes the daily dinner, fish and chips is a real winner.

Arguments here and arguments there,
'Mum, I'm going to a party, what shall I wear?'

Shower or wash and night wear on, then it's not long
before they're gone.

Up the wooden hill they climb, every night in single line.

Snuggled up they look so sweet, Mum feels run off her feet.

Then I sit down with a nice cup of tea,
I sigh and think well that's life with my three!

My children are getting all my attention,
not polishing, cleaning and all the other things I could mention.

In my life they wait until last, just because children grow fast.

And in years to come I'd sit and wonder, why I made such a blunder.

Not playing and enjoying them while they're little,
just through elbow grease and spittle.

So if you come in and think a bomb has landed,
just think of the many children who are stranded.

No love or understanding do they receive,
I know it sounds so hard to believe.

I love my children they are the best,
so in years to come I'll look back while taking a well earned
Rest!

Sally Osborne

WHERE?

I think of you but you're not there
to take my call.
Don't you care?
I cannot see you, strange to say
to laugh and gossip
on a summer's day.
Who can I tell all my troubles to,
now that you've gone,
Inconsiderate you!
So talk to me now, a voice in my head
I'll try to hear clearly
just what you said.
Where are you now that your spirit is free;
can you shop till you drop
in eternity?
Do you see all your children here on earth
as they laugh in the sunshine
and splash in the surf.
Are you beside them night and day
reach out and touch
just a kiss away.
Are you part of the shadows in evening glow
or a rustle in leaves
as the winds gently blow.
Maybe I could visit your spiritual place
and for one special moment
we'd come face to face.
Be part of the rainbow that arcs above
sleep softly dear friend
with all my love.

Gillian Goss

A Wife's Lament

It's one of those days, I'm at sixes and sevens
The sky's gone grey, it's going to pour from the heavens
What can I do, shall I sit down and rest
Or just keep on going, doing my best

Housework, shopping, it's all got to be done
Washing and ironing, not what I'd call fun
But what can I do, shall I make myself tea
And then start tackling this dull drudgery

My brain's working overtime, the baby wants fed
Then he needs a bath and putting to bed
There's dirty dishes piling up in the sink
I've got to sit down, have a minute to think

Cooking and scrubbing 'til I'd like to scream
I'd like to wake up, find it's all a bad dream
But what can I do, it's all got to be done
I wish I could run and escape to the sun

Marie Angela Bridgen

NEVER

What will you look like as you grow older?
I can only think, as your ashes grow colder.
Never to hear you cry, 'Mummy and Daddy.'
Never to tell you, 'I love you madly.'

Never to see you smile and cry,
Never to wave you 'Goodbye.'
Never to cuddle you on your days that are down.
Never to see you angry and frown.

Never to cook for you, or change your nappy.
Never to tell you when you've been wrong, or see you happy.
Never to sing 'Happy birthday' and blow out your candles.
Never to buy you a new pair of sandals.

Never to see you start at school.
Never to see you acting the fool.
Never to hear your footsteps as you walk.
Never, ever to hear you talk.

Never to see you leave your food.
Never to see you in a mood.
Never to see you love or hate.
Never to see you with a mate.

Never to tuck you in bed at night.
Never to switch off your bedroom light.
Never to iron the clothes for you to wear.
Never to wash and comb your hair.

Never to nurse your hurt and grazed knee.
Never to see your presents, opened with glee.
Never to sing you a nursery rhyme.
Never to see you grow up in time.

Only to see you born asleep.
And for you to see us forever weep.

Christina Redfearn

FRIENDSHIP LOVE WILL NEVER DIE

When you love someone
And you know it's right,
When you're near them
You wont let them out of your sight,
But what do you do when your feelings change?
There is no one there for me to blame,
As time goes by you wonder why?
You remember when you thought,
Your love would never die.
What I'm saying is this is how I feel.
My love for you
Is no longer real.
I know deep down my feelings are dead,
But the memories I still have are here in my head,
What we had was special,
But it's time we both move on.
Although we don't love each other,
I know our friendship feelings will always be strong.
Please forgive me, or at least please try
Because my friendship love will never die.

Becky Morris

TREADMILL

Toys and books scattered, it's all quite a mess.
When I'll be finished is anyone's guess!
Children asleep - tucked up in bed,
Rusty the rabbit, cat and dog fed,
Pots on the sink ready to dry.
Large piles of ironing stands a foot high.
Food for tomorrow, I should now prepare.
Lunch box for school - coins for the fare.
But finish I do, and lay down my head.
Alarm set for six and I'm snuggled in bed.
It doesn't take long to drift off to sleep.
I certainly don't need to start counting sheep!
Another day dawns, I start over again,
Children to see to - the office by ten.
Shopping at lunch time - no time to eat,
The day passes by - 'My poor little feet.'
Children to meet as they come out of school.
Time left for me - 'Don't be a fool!'

Elizabeth Gray

A WOMAN'S THOUGHTS

The year was nineteen forty-six, when I arrived on earth,
Although it was quite difficult, my mother gave me birth.

The only grandchild of both sides, my family's kith and kin,
Because their love was priceless, I was surely going to win.

In the beginning of the fifties was the time I started school,
I learned to read and write and then, to learn about the rule.

The rule they taught me every day was behave yourself and care,
Because I was an only child, I was told to always share.

Then became the sixties, what fun did I enjoy,
Music, dancing, make-up perhaps to meet a boy.

By the time it was the seventies, I was married and had my son,
My little boy with golden hair, now a different kind of fun.

Then I had my daughter, the sweetest little pearl,
Heaven had been good to me, a boy and now a girl.

At the beginning of the eighties, I had my best surprise,
Heaven gave me another gift, my son with big blue eyes.

Now I had my family, to care and help them grow,
They say the flowers that you reap are from the seeds you sow.

Through all the nineties I have seen these beautiful flowers bloom,
Their colour, shape and perfume can brighten any gloom.

Looking through those fifty years, on the journey of my life,
My roles have been a daughter, a mother and a wife.

The year is now two thousand and forward is the key,
A grandma now and middle-aged, what's the future hold for me?

The future no one knows about, I'll have to wait and see,
But reminiscing over all those years, life has been alright for me.

B Hattersley

FAT FREE WORLD

100% fat free
Diet magazines aimed at teens
Looking at every girl I see
To try and find out if she's skinnier than me.

What's this obsession with being thin?
What's so sexy about bones
Poking through the skin?
Why do I think dieting's the way to win?

Supermodels, skin and bone
On my plate a rice cake sits, alone,
While I pray that soon I'll lose a stone
Let's not think what'll happen if I don't.

Rhiannon Moore (15)

WHY WAIT

Why wait for the sound of a closing door,
the silence that follows tense and raw.

Why wait for the sound of the telephone ring,
watching and waiting for it to offer up its monotonous tone.

Collect your thoughts, stench the flow of self pity and hurt
he won't be coming home.

Quickly bathe, shampoo and dress;
collect your thoughts, your bag and yes!

Take up the offer of last week's date,
this one's not coming back, so why wait!

Marjie Bagnall

REFLECTION

Her bones stiff and her eyesight poor,
She fumbled for the handle of the heavy oak door.
Long, thin fingers stroked fine white hair
And her lungs coughed resentment in the musty air.

The river of mirror was smooth and cool.
She watched the lined face in the shining pool.
Old eyes closed against the picture in the glass,
The darkness inside was a passageway to the past.

The childhood age was the furthest gone.
A world in which she had belonged.
A thousand summers of climbing trees
And flying kites on the warm sea breeze.

She remembered the years of broken hearts.
Precious dreams in a million parts.
So many different versions of the same song,
Unsure of what was right and what was wrong.

A special day of pearls and silk.
Flowing streams of satin milk.
Coloured windows, tall grey towers,
Love, laughter and ivory flowers.

Her journey entered a different role
When she breathed life into another soul.
Giggles, wriggles and tumbles down the stair.
Seeking when she knew there was a child behind the chair.

Another special day of gaining a son.
Her veiled daughter had a new life begun.
The next generation would follow soon.
Sunshine faded, light came only from the moon.

Life's greatest love could not stay forever,
One day soon they would again be together.
Tired eyes opened, the image was gone.
The gilt-edged mirror still shimmered and shone.

Kimberley Clark

BATTERED WIFE

For him
She
Bore child
Washed clothes
Ironed shirts
Cooked meals
Took slaps, blows
Drunken rages
Accusations
Other women
Black eyes
Suffered silence
Grew wise
Packed bags
Kept
Her mind.

Madeline Keyes

A DAY WITH MY TWINS

Up at six or seven each day,
   Sort the twins, who just want to play,
No lie-ins at the weekends, nor week days,
   Time has no meaning for these little rays,
Breakfast is next, oh what a mess,
   Cornflakes everywhere, they do try, oh bless,
Now they are happy, watching the box,
   I can get on and wash the crocks,
Next clean the house and make the beds,
   I wish I could rest my weary head,
But no, they are quiet, what are they up to,
   The aquarium's been attacked, the fish in a stew,
Time to get out and shop for supplies,
   The twins on board, and I get stereo cries,
Hassled and stressed, I make for home,
   Pushchair so loaded, it gives a groan,
Once at home, I soon can tell,
   Two nappies need changing, oh what a smell,
Feeding is next and then for their rest,
   While I do the washing to keep abreast,
Soon awake and hungry, they push toys aside,
   They sit ready and waiting, with mouths open wide,
Then comes play time, with balls and bricks,
   And I get away with one bruise from their kicks,
Bath time is next, bubbles galore,
   Most of the water ends up on the floor,
They are such happy bundles of joy,
   But they don't half know how to be coy,
Time for bed, story and chimes, snuggled up close, so sublime,
   With not a care in the world, and those twins are mine.

Jenny Jones

LETTING GO

When we are blessed with children
They are not ours alone
We have them for a little while
To help them until they are grown.

We feed and clean them carefully
We bathe and change the nappy
We get up nights to soothe and hold
As babies they're quite happy.

Then we reach the school age
We have to loosen our hold
We've taught our children to be kind
Thoughtful, considerate and bold.

Next it's off to high school.
And you face the dreaded teens.
It's all loud music, untidy rooms,
And holes in faded jeans.

When you think of the things you pass onto your child
The qualities others find endearing
Their friendship and love are given elsewhere
It's natural for you to be fearing.

Never be frightened of letting them go
Don't worry that you may lose them
They find their partners, you've given them the heart
The confidence they need to choose them.

You won't lose your family by letting go
Your circle of loved ones will grow
You will be richer and happier by far
I did it: It works: I know.

Ann Tyas

SCANS AND MAMS!

My daughter's just called, she's had one of those scans,
She's expecting her first did you know?
Isn't it marvellous the things they can see
Going on in her tum down below?

The babe is so clear, even sucking its thumb
And it's kicking and turning around.
The parents both watch fascinated to see
That all parts of their baby are sound.

They can even have 'photos' but I don't think *I* would,
It's stretching things rather too far -
I wonder if we'd had these things in our day
We'd have wanted to see all *our* star?

Still, science, technology, working this way
Can only be all to the good,
But it's clinical too and the mystery is gone,
I wonder, do *you* think that it should?

Paddy Jupp

THE CROSS (A DREAM)

The beautiful shining cross,
How lovely it stands on high,
On top of a lonely mountain,
Lifted up to the sky.

Pointing people onwards,
Never pointing down,
So it's up a thorny mountain,
If you wish to win a crown.

There seems no path to follow,
It's all so rough with thorns,
But look at the prize at the top
Behind that cross of gold.

Jesus stands behind it,
Looking down on those,
Who attempt to climb it,
Sorrowing if they fall.

Golden gates are open,
For those who get to the top,
And his dear face to greet you,
And to lead you on.

So please don't stop or falter,
Go on and persevere,
Just think what's at the top,
Through the golden gateway dear.

Jesus, 'The king of glory'
Who died so long ago
Is so bright in glory,
His white robes are turned blue.

So, follow the Saviour, dear ones.
That dear golden cross so bright.
Though the path be rough and dreary,
Follow on with all your might.

Violet Mattinson

WHEN YOU BECOME AN EX

When you become an ex
It's maybe not so good
It's the battle of the sex
And it's easy to be rude

To pick on all the things
That you didn't really think
Were bad habits in another
They could drive you to the brink

It's easy to forget
The good times that you shared
Easy to put behind you
The fact you ever cared

When did things start to go bad
Do you ever really know
It's the things that make you so sad
That make you want to go

But what about the good times
Have the memories all died
When you spent your time a-laughing
And you never ever sighed

It takes two to make a future
It takes two to make things last
But it only takes the one of you
To make the present past

When couples start to break up
They do nothing else but fight
It's sad that when they move on
They see that they could have got it right

S R Potter

LONELINESS

The house is full
Laughter all round
But if your heart's lonely
You will hear no sound.
Locked in your own private world
Wrapped up in your own private thoughts
Lost is the key that opens your heart
And with it no love to hold
Life's an empty shell
Waiting to be filled
With loving care and tenderness
To take away the loneliness
Friends and relations gather round
But still there is no sound.

K Morris

MY MOM
(For Sheelah Carpenter)

I feel so proud to have you,
And to say that you're my mom,
The love and warmth you always give,
Is undoubtedly second to none.

I'm sure that people who know you,
Are really pleased they do,
You're a truly remarkable woman,
And I hope to be like you.

There are no words to express,
Exactly how I feel,
But deep inside, I know I can't hide,
How loved you make me feel.

I know that being a good mother,
Is a difficult job to do,
But I know I'm already halfway there,
With a role model just like you.

The bond between mother and daughter,
Isn't just about family ties,
It's of love, trust and many more things,
That you have helped me find.

A woman can fit into any role,
Just flitting from one to the other,
But there's only one thing you are to me,
And that is my dearest mother.

Samantha Wood

BRIEF ENCOUNTER

We touched but briefly, you and I my love,
A momentary glow and then it died.
We had no future, you and I my love,
Two strangers passing in the night, we cried,
For all the things that might have been, my love,
But never could be ours, although we tried.

I met your eyes across the street, my love,
I saw a spark, reflected there from mine.
It touched the bottom of my heart, my love,
Two souls reached out, two hearts entwined,
Then all the love I had was yours, my love,
And all the love you had was mine.

We knew we had too many ties, my love,
Too many strings wound round our hearts
Too many things to leave behind, my love,
We always knew we had to part.
A burst of glory gone too soon, my love,
I'll always keep you in my heart.

And now I see you in the street, my love,
You smile at me and it's in vain,
My heart is breaking when we meet, my love,
I know we'll never be together again,
I whisper low, I love you so, my love.
And go on walking in the rain.

Margaret Helliwell

MEMORIAL DAY

I walked the quiet hallowed ground
Where slurried children sleep.
Laid to rest with scarce a sound
Their shock and grief too deep
Their crosses stood like sentinels
Breeze blew like gentle sighs.
Across the valley chapel bells
Rang in my ears, my eyes
Were misted, full of unshed tears.
I saw them all at play
I swear, among their carefree peers
On that memorial day.
Young voices called in clear true notes
As only children can,
Unclogged by coal dust, trilling throats,
The lost of Aberfan.
Sweet laughter rang around the stones
And echoed vibrantly.
Dark doubt lies buried with their bones,
Who breathed new life in me.

Mair Patchett

YOUTH IN AGE

Feet swollen with time's bloat fail on the stairs.
Mind, active still, with patience pays for rent
Corporeal weakness. Acceptance buys content
And refuge for the body time impairs
Yet still seeks to be used. Beneath the layers
Of wrinkles, fingers gnarled and skilled are lent
To simpler tasks, or furled, work done. Frame, spent,
Narrows to the implacable cage of wheeled chairs.

Yet in her mind she skips in spring again;
The years depart, falling like autumn leaves.
Restored she walks in youth along the lane
Where yet her memory treads. Remembrance weaves
A solace for her age. Remote, serene, and mild
She seems untroubled, carefree. Like a child.

Sara Goodwins

THE LONG WAY HOME

Once upon a time, a hundred years ago
A man and his wife were trudging through the snow
The wind started blowing, the snow got in their eyes
'I'm glad that we left early and said all our goodbyes.'

On and on they trudged, they came across a cave
'Quick let's slip in here,' he said, 'Ooh! I wish you would behave.'
They built a little fire and tried to settle down
They had a little cuddle, her husband he just frowned

They made it nice and cosy, a real little home from home
She said 'It's luverley 'ere! I wish I'd brought me gnome.'
'We'll wait in here 'til the snow storm clears,'
'Eh! What?' she said and boxed him round the ears

Her husband he just stood there, wondering what he'd done
So she crept up right behind him and kicked him up the bum
He said 'Now hold on dear' and clipped her round the ear
'I think if you look outside the storm's beginning to clear.'

'Shall we make a move then,' 'My legs are beginning to buckle.'
'Yes, let's make haste!' 'Do what?' she said and rapped him
                                              on the knuckle
'I can't take much more of this, I'm feeling rather poor'
'What do you expect my dear when we only live next door.'

G Ryan

A Mother

A mother is someone precious
To be treasured with loving care,
The miss of her you'll never know
Until you see that empty chair.

When you thought she was nagging
And she never understood you,
That was only because she cared,
Only time proves that was true.

There's many things we can replace
In this uncertain world we live,
But a mother is irreplaceable
With that endless love she gives.

Jinty Wicks

BONDS OF GOLD

I held out my hand for my friends to see,
The trinket my mum had bought for me
A little gold ring, oh what a treasure,
To this small girl, it brought great pleasure.

No glove was worn though the hand was blue
My engagement ring from my love so true,
It fluttered and sparkled, so all could see,
Three bright diamonds, you'd given to me.

Next my wedding, a band of gold
Continued tradition from days of old
We made our vows, one to another
And promised to be, friend and lover.

When my grandmother died, I was given her ring
And all the memories it was bound to bring,
It's always so good, to see it there
And know it's another thing we share.

And now I have granddaughters of my own
In years to come when they're fully grown
I hope they'll have happy thoughts like mine,
When I leave them my own rings in time.

Phyllis Henderson

DREAMS

I close my eyes and start to dream,
Of a place I have not seen,
With golden sands, palm trees so high,
They look as though they touch the sky.
Deep blue sea and pale blue sky,
Ships sailing silent in the night.
Planes taking off in flight.
Cool sea breeze blowing on my face,
Will I ever see this place.
Then I awake, what do I see,
The one place
I will always be.

Dinkie

Tomorrow's Another New Day

I woke up early one morning
When the day had just begun
Lying in bed I looked through the window
And just caught sight of the sun.

I felt it was wrong to be lying in bed
On such a lovely, bright, sunny day
So I quickly arose, donned my old gardening clothes
And promptly downstairs made my way.

I decided to stay in the garden,
Working until mid-day
When the sun would be at its hottest
And too hot for me to stay.

My plan was good and worked very well
I was getting what I wanted to do done
There was just one task left that I needed to do
When a big black cloud came and blocked out the sun.

I went back indoors, not a moment too soon
For the cloud I had seen brought some rain.
There were loud claps of thunder and lightning as well
How long it would last there was no way to tell.

But there's always tomorrow and what it will bring
And whatever that is will be new
So let us not fritter our whole lives away
Wondering what tomorrow will bring us to do.

When tomorrow arrives - as it most surely will -
Let us do what needs doing with zest
And not worry or fret or get very upset
If we can honestly say
'Well, I did do my best
And tomorrow's another new day.'

Peggy C

LET OUR MARRIAGE AND ME GO

Why are you doing this?
You can't keep playing mind games.
You're bringing me down.
Now I've got to fight back!
We've had twenty-five years.
That's a quarter century.
You haven't cared or tried or helped.
It's only now I've walked away,
You decide you can't live without me.
We've been dying for a long time.
Just lay our marriage to rest,
It's the only way to go.
You need help, there's no doubt about that,
You're still not trying to help yourself.
I can't carry you anymore.
My love has died,
Please let it rest in peace.

Caroline Quinn

Full Circle

Teens to twenties, I'm such a smart thing
Earning my living, wearing the latest thing
I love my job and I love the money
This must be the land of milk and honey
It's a fabulous life!

Twenties to thirties, whatever has happened?
A man and two infants waiting to be fattened
I'm cooking and feeding and cooking again
Life is certainly not quite the same
It's a hard old life!

Forties to fifties, they've all left the nest
I'm typing and computing along with the best
I'm really smart now, smarter than ever before
Life should be great but . . . what am I searching for?
It's a funny old life!

Mid-fifties to sixties and again I am grounded
Grandchildren have arrived, all cute, fat and rounded
Mum needs to work so here I'll remain
Cooking and feeding all over again
Then I look at each innocent open loving face
And I know what was missing in those forty-ish days
It's a fabulous life!

Pat Holloway

RAINDROPS

The torrent of hormones
We must bear
The onslaught of puberty
Spots and pubic hair

Pre-menstrual syndrome
Cravings and needs
Cuddles and chocolate
And understanding please!

Swirls of creativity
Ebb and flow, amongst
The emotional highs and lows.

Ovulation, copulation . . . pregnancy!
A woman's amazing
Gift to conceive.

Labour is hard, but necessity
A journey from womb
To reality!

Overwhelming feelings of love and pride
Blanket you from the world outside
Your special moment
Forever in time.

And what of the menopause
That which we fear
The shedding of fertility
May raise a tear.

You've finished the roller coaster
Of hormonal swings
You have balance, stability
Enjoy what it brings!

Kate Rees

SUBMISSIONS INVITED
SOMETHING FOR EVERYONE

WOMENSWORDS 2001 - Strictly women, have your say the female way!

POETRY NOW 2001 - Any subject, any style, any time.

STRONGWORDS 2001 - Warning! Age restriction, must be between 16-24, opinionated and have strong views. (Not for the faint-hearted)

All poems no longer than 30 lines.
Always welcome! No fee!
Cash Prizes to be won!

Mark your envelope (eg Poetry Now) *2001*
Send to: Forward Press Ltd
Remus House, Coltsfoot Drive,
Peterborough, PE2 9JX

OVER £10,000 POETRY PRIZES TO BE WON!
Judging will take place in October 2001